Play
1, 2, 3, 4, 5

written by Anne Giulieri

photography by Ned Meldrum

Look at the boys and girls.

2

They are playing games.

3

Can you play games at school?

4

Look at your hand.
You can play 1, 2, 3, 4, 5
games at school!

Hiding Games

You can play hiding games.

You can hide in the garden.

Chocolate Banana Pops

by Anne Giulieri

Chocolate Banana Pops

GRL: E **Nonfiction**

Word count: 131

Curriculum link: me/family, science

Text type: procedural

High frequency words introduced:
fun, onto, today, with;
make (academic)

High frequency words consolidated:
get, inside, like, they

Example inferential questions:
- *Why do you think the little girl is putting the sticks in the banana?*
- *Why is the chocolate put in the microwave? What will happen to it?*

Phonological awareness/graphophonics:
initial consonant digraphs 'ch', 'th';
onset and rime 'p-op', 'r-ed', 'c-ut',
'g-et', 'h-ot'; initial consonant blends
'st', 'br'; suffixes 's', 'ing'; compound
words 'today', 'inside', 'onto'; initial
letter names/sounds

Program links:
Chocolate Banana Pops E-Book
Bananas in My Tummy (F)
Digital Poster *'Bananas'*

You can hide
in the playground.

You can hide
inside a tunnel.

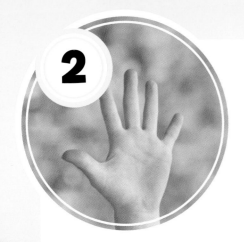

Playground Games

You can play
playground games.

You can go
on the slide.

You can jump
off the log.

You can go
on the bars.

9

Garden Games

You can play garden games.

You can look
at the big leaves.

Can you see a butterfly?

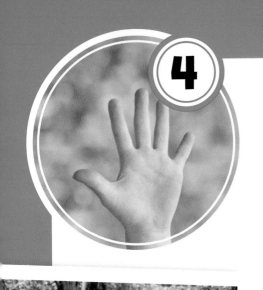

Running and Jumping Games

You can play running and jumping games. Where can you run and jump at school?

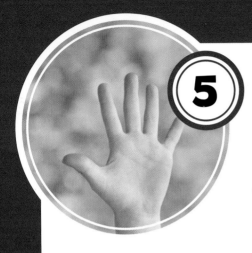

5 Sitting Games

You can play sitting games.

14

You can sit
and look
at a book.

You can sit and draw.

Look at your hand.
You can play
1, 2, 3, 4, 5 games.